Software Development for GxP Regulated Industries

Deliver GxP Compliance Software in an Agile Way

Adrian Krzesniak

Contents

1. Introduction

Software development for GxP-regulated companies involves additional requirements, including specific guidelines from EU Annex 11, and FDA CFR Part 11. These requirements cover aspects such as electronic signatures, audit trails, data integrity, and more. Due to the stringent regulations governing GxP-regulated companies, software and system suppliers must adhere to established rules and procedures for developing, releasing, implementing, and maintaining software.

When validation or pre-validation is needed, this book explains how to implement agile validation by embedding the validation process within the development cycle, rather than using the traditional V-Model validation based on the waterfall approach.

In this book, you will find valuable information to help you develop and make software attractive from a compliance point of view for GxP-regulated industries, including pharmaceuticals, laboratories, clinical trials, and the broader life sciences sector.

You will also find numerous tips on how a software development vendor can prepare for a supplier audit conducted by a GxP-regulated company.

2. Understanding GxP regulations

2.1. What is GxP?

GxP stands for "Good Practice" and is a general term that encompasses various regulations and guidelines designed to ensure that products are safe, meet their intended use, and adhere to quality standards. The "x" in GxP can be replaced with different letters to specify the type of practice, such as Good Manufacturing Practice (GMP), Good Laboratory Practice (GLP), and Good Clinical Practice (GCP).

2.1.1. Key components of GxP

Good Manufacturing Practice (GMP)

GMP guidelines ensure that products are consistently produced and controlled according to quality standards. These practices are crucial in the manufacturing of pharmaceuticals, medical devices, and food products.

Key aspects include proper documentation, validation, and quality control.

Good Laboratory Practice (GLP):

➢ GLP regulations govern the conduct of non-clinical laboratory studies. These practices ensure the integrity and reliability of laboratory data, which is essential for the safety assessment of products.
➢ GLP covers aspects such as study planning, data recording, and reporting.

Good Clinical Practice (GCP):

➢ GCP guidelines are designed to ensure the ethical and scientific quality of clinical trials involving human subjects. These practices protect the rights, safety, and well-being of trial participants.

➢ GCP includes requirements for trial design, conduct, monitoring, and reporting.

2.1.2. GxP in software development

In the pharmaceutical, life sciences, and other regulated industries, software systems must comply with GxP regulations to ensure data integrity, product quality, and patient safety.

2.1.3. Regulatory bodies and guidelines

Several regulatory bodies oversee GxP compliance, which regulated companies are responsible for, including:

➢ U.S. Food and Drug Administration (FDA): Provides guidelines and regulations for GMP, GLP, and GCP.
➢ European Medicines Agency (EMA): Offers similar guidelines for the European Union.
➢ International Council for Harmonization (ICH): Develops global standards for GxP practices.

2.1.4. Impact of GxP on software development

GxP regulations impose specific requirements on both software vendors and regulated companies, such as those in the pharmaceutical, biotech, and laboratory sectors.

Regulated companies

- Vendors must be selected based on their ability to pass official qualifications, which may include undergoing audits.
- Ensure that vendors accept GxP conditions for delivering and maintaining software, typically outlined in a Service Level Agreement (SLA).
- Have the right to periodically audit software vendors to ensure compliance with standards.

Software/System vendors:

- Establish and adhere to procedures for planning, developing, implementing, and maintaining software.
- Incorporate GxP requirements into the software to ensure it meets validation standards for use in regulated environments

2.2. Computer system validation

Computer System Validation (CSV), referred to here as "validation," is the process of ensuring that computer systems used in regulated industries, such as pharmaceuticals and biotechnology, consistently produce accurate and reliable results that comply with regulatory requirements. This involves a series of documented activities that demonstrate the system's ability to perform its intended functions correctly and consistently.

Key aspects of CSV include

- Planning: Defining the scope, objectives, and approach for validation.

- ➢ Requirements specification: Documenting user and functional requirements.
- ➢ Risk assessment: Identifying and mitigating potential risks.
- ➢ Testing: Conducting various tests to verify system functionality, performance, and security.
- ➢ Documentation: Maintaining comprehensive records of validation activities and results.
- ➢ Change control: Managing changes to the system to ensure continued compliance.
- ➢ Review and approval: Ensuring validation activities are reviewed and approved by qualified personnel.

CSV ensures that computer systems are fit for their intended use and comply with industry standards and regulations, thereby safeguarding product quality and patient safety.

2.3. Regulatory goals

The primary goals of GxP regulations are to ensure that products are safe for use, meet quality standards, and are produced in a controlled environment. These regulations help maintain public trust and protect patients' safety by:

- ➢ Safeguarding product quality: Ensuring that products are consistently produced to high standards.
- ➢ Ensuring patient safety: Protecting patients from harmful or ineffective products.
- ➢ Maintaining data integrity: Ensuring that all data related to product development and testing is accurate and reliable.

By understanding and implementing GxP regulations, software development companies can create software that not only complies with regulatory requirements but also improves product quality and ensures patient safety.

2.4. Audit perspective

Since software development suppliers will be audited by GxP regulated companies, it is crucial to understand the nature of these audits and the expectations involved. These audits ensure that suppliers comply with regulatory standards and maintain the integrity of their software systems.

Key aspects of GxP audits

➢ Compliance verification: Audits verify that software development processes adhere to GxP regulations, including guidelines from Annex 11 and FDA CFR Part 11. This includes checking for proper documentation, electronic signatures, audit trails, and data integrity measures.
➢ Quality assurance: Audits assess the quality management systems in place, ensuring that software is developed, tested, and maintained according to high standards. This includes reviewing procedures for risk management, change control, and incident management.
➢ Periodic reviews: Regular audits ensure ongoing compliance and continuous improvement. They help identify areas for enhancement and ensure that vendors keep up with evolving regulatory requirements.

➤ Documentation and records: Audits review the completeness and accuracy of documentation related to software development.

Importance of GxP vendor audits

Understanding and preparing for GxP vendor audits is essential for software development suppliers. These audits not only ensure compliance but also enhance the credibility and reliability of the software. By adhering to GxP standards, suppliers can build trust with regulated companies and contribute to the overall safety and quality of products in the life sciences sector.

3. Software development in GxP environments

Developing software for GxP-regulated environments requires adherence to stringent guidelines and standards to ensure compliance, data integrity, and product quality. This chapter outlines the software development lifecycle (SDLC) tailored for GxP-regulated industries, highlighting key processes and best practices.

The entire approach to software development needs to be described in the procedure. This procedure must be followed during software development and will be audited during supplier audits.

3.1. Planning and requirements gathering

The first phase of the SDLC involves thorough planning and requirements gathering. This step is crucial for understanding the specific needs of the GxP-regulated environment and ensuring that all regulatory requirements are addressed.

Requirements specifications

Requirements Specifications (RS): This artifact captures user needs and expectations, detailing the functionalities the software must provide. Requirements can be structured as traditional specifications or framed within an agile context, such as epics, features, and user stories.

Some companies choose to use only agile requirements, such as features and user stories. Others prefer to create requirements in a standard form, sometimes as document files, or define them in a requirements management tool and then link them, for example, to features or user stories.

Although software development vendors typically prefer requirements in the form of features and user stories, regulated companies may request standard requirements specifications with classic requirements. Therefore, it's beneficial to have such a version available just in case.

Audit tips

For auditors, it is crucial that the vendor manages requirements in any form or shape and can demonstrate which requirements were introduced in each version of the software. Additionally, it is important to ensure that these requirements are covered by testing and can be presented in the form of a requirements traceability matrix.

3.2. Design and architecture

Once the requirements are gathered, the next phase is designing software architecture. This outlines how the software will be structured and how it will meet the specified requirements.

➢ System Design Specifications (SDS): Detailed design documents that describe the software architecture.
➢ Data flow diagrams: Visual representations of data movement within the system.
➢ Security design: Ensuring data integrity and incorporating security measures.

Documentation can be stored as markdown documents in a source code management tool, allowing developers to easily review and comment on the architecture and system design. Supporting diagrams, including those that show data flow, are crucial for maintaining data integrity.

Audit tips

For auditors, it is essential to ensure that the system has a comprehensive design, with well-defined data flows and security measures. These aspects should be discussed and reviewed by multiple subject matter experts (SMEs) to ensure thorough consideration.

3.3. Software development

In the past, companies needed to follow strict waterfall and V-model methodologies to demonstrate to regulated industries that they adhered to best practices.

Nowadays, suppliers can use methods that suit them best. Many companies use agile methodologies, specifically Scrum, as their software development framework. They utilize modern IDEs, source code control systems, and CI/CD processes to deliver value to customers faster than ever. Infrastructure as code and cloud architecture further accelerate this process.

In Scrum, iterative development, continuous integration, and collaboration are fundamental to agile development. Although Agile promotes working software over documentation, documentation remains very important for GxP software.

Reviews

Code reviews, along with design and requirements reviews, are vital components of the development process. The procedure should clearly outline how these reviews are to be conducted. Additionally, it is important to ensure that evidence of these reviews is readily available to auditors upon request. Reviews are typically performed using a source code management tool. Remember that regulated companies rely on these reviews, as they are unable to conduct them themselves.

Audit tips

The software development process should be documented in a procedure that is approved and adhered to. The supplier, or the company developing the software, needs to provide evidence that this procedure is being followed.

3.4. Testing

Testing is critical to ensure the software meets all requirements formed as user stories and performs as intended. This phase involves rigorous testing to identify and fix any issues.

- ➤ Unit testing: Testing individual components/ methods of the software.
- ➤ Integration testing: Ensuring different components work together seamlessly.
- ➤ User Acceptance Testing (UAT): Confirming the software meets user needs.
- ➤ System testing: Testing the entire system against requirements.

Risk-based testing in GxP

Risk-based testing in GxP environments focuses on identifying and prioritizing potential risks to patient safety, product quality, and data integrity. This approach ensures that testing efforts are concentrated on the most critical areas, optimizing resource allocation and enhancing compliance. By leveraging risk assessments, companies can tailor their testing strategies to address high-risk components, thereby improving the reliability and effectiveness of GxP computerized systems.

Quality Assurance (QA) role

It is essential to include the role of QA as part of the software development team, extending typical Scrum roles. In many scenarios, this can be a tester or testers with an extended role. For larger software projects, a separate role of QA manager may be required. The QA role is responsible for ensuring that development follows written procedures, implements and tests GxP requirements, and verifies that all required artifacts related to validation and release are delivered. This role is additional to typical Scrum roles but is crucial for development in GxP companies and agile validation.

QA can also be the person who hosts supplier audits and explains how the process works within the company.

QA is also responsible for conducting internal periodic audits to ensure that software development complies with defined procedures.

Audit tips

All requirements should be tested and tracked using a Requirements Traceability Matrix (RTM), which can be generated as an Excel table or with any available tool. Additionally, a risk-based testing approach helps focus on three critical GxP elements: product quality, patient safety, and data integrity.

	Requirement #1	Requirement #2	Requirement #3	Requirement #4	Requirement #5	⋮
Test Case #1	Risk #1		Risk #2			
Test Case #2						
Test Case #3		Risk #3				
Test Case #4						
Test Case #5				Risk #5		
...			...			

Example of a Requirements Traceability Matrix (RTM)

3.5. Cybersecurity

Pharmaceutical and other GxP-regulated companies are increasingly focusing on cybersecurity. It is essential to update vulnerable libraries, perform penetration testing, and check code for vulnerabilities. This process should be clearly defined as a procedure to ensure consistency and thoroughness. Regular audits and reviews should be conducted to verify compliance with cybersecurity standards. Additionally, training programs for staff on cybersecurity best practices can help mitigate risks and enhance overall security posture.

Audit tips

It is important to demonstrate that the supplier prioritizes cybersecurity, which has become increasingly critical for pharmaceutical companies following several cyber-attacks. Suppliers should show evidence of proactive measures, such as regular updates to vulnerable libraries, comprehensive penetration testing, and thorough code reviews to identify and mitigate vulnerabilities. Additionally, having a well-defined cybersecurity procedure and conducting regular training for staff in the best practices can further enhance security. Auditors should look for documentation and proof of these activities to ensure that cybersecurity is a top priority.

3.6. Release

Once the software has been thoroughly tested and all documentation is prepared, it is time to release the software. Each software release should be assigned a unique release number.

The release represents the final milestone in the development process, serving as a comprehensive check to ensure all requirements are fulfilled, tests are completed, and all necessary documentation, including technical and user manuals, is in place. The release should be finalized with detailed release notes, summarizing the changes, improvements, and any known issues.

Audit tips

The official release is crucial for regulated customers, as it allows them to classify the software as GAMP category 4, like off-the-shelf software. This classification simplifies the computer system validation process. Additionally, the version number is important as a reference for other change control activities, ensuring traceability and accountability. Auditors should verify that the release process includes comprehensive documentation, such as release notes, and that all requirements, tests, and necessary manuals are finalized and available.

3.7. Delivery & implementation

There should be a plan to deliver software by the supplier, agreed upon with the regulated company. An important aspect is that all knowledge gathered during implementation should be transferred from the project team to the operations team to facilitate validation.

Training the users

Another crucial topic is delivering training to users. Initially, this can be in the form of train-the-trainer sessions to educate key users, who can then train others within the organization. The focus should be on providing training for key users and administrators. Trained users can take an active role in validating the system. Without proper training on how to use the system, its GxP intended use cannot be proven.

Hypercare

It is good practice for the supplier to act as the first line of support during the initial three-month period to assist key users in operating the system. Besides training, key users need to become fluent in operating the computerized system.

Audit tips

Without a well-defined implementation plan, it is difficult to achieve the intended use of the system, which is a key aspect of readiness for system/software validation and going live. The system must be fully operational and validated to cover the regulated company's business processes.

3.8. Validation

There is a common misconception that suppliers can validate their own software and provide validation certificates. Only GxP-regulated companies can perform software validation, as they are the only ones who can demonstrate the intended use of the software within their specific operating environment.

However, it is important for companies delivering software to pre-validate the software for their standard configurations, known as blueprints. In some cases, pre-validation can help regulated software companies reduce their validation effort by focusing on changes to configurations. This pre-validation can be performed using automated testing scripts or traditional scripts.

The validation should focus on:

➢ Checking the installation and configuration of the software.
➢ Verifying critical functionalities related to business functions as well as typical GxP functions such as audit trails, printing, signatures, and user assignments.
➢ Testing user scenarios reflect normal use of the software.

More information about validation and the use of agile validation can be found in Chapter 5

Audit tips

Pre-validation demonstrates that the vendor is experienced in working with GxP-regulated companies and understands their requirements and specifics. This can be a significant selling point for the software vendor.

3.9. Maintenance

Maintenance is critical for maintaining the computer system in validated state. Expect the regulated company will need SLA with vendor to agree all aspects on maintenance dependence of system.

Incident Management

Regulated companies should have a system in place to create tickets in case the software doesn't work. The response time and all criteria related to support should be described in the Service Level Agreement (SLA). This system should ensure timely resolution of issues, with clear communication channels between the vendor and the customer.

Additionally, an escalation process should be defined to handle incidents that are not resolved within the agreed-upon timeframe. This process should specify the steps to escalate the issue to higher levels of support, including management involvement if necessary. Regular monitoring and reporting on incident management performance can help maintain high standards of service and quickly address any recurring problems.

Change control

Since the system is validated, maintenance releases with bug fixes need to be delivered in a controlled manner. Directly pushing fixes to the validated environment of a regulated company is not allowed.

Before updating to a new version of the software with fixes as a maintenance release, a sandbox environment should be established. This allows the regulated company to prepare their change control based on the new release notes and validate the new changes and fixes.

Audit tips

Without regular maintenance, every system will quickly fall out of its validated state. It is the responsibility of regulated companies to ensure systems remain validated through ongoing maintenance. Increasingly, this maintenance is performed in collaboration with software and computerized system vendors, especially as software becomes more cloud-based and more complex to deploy and maintain.

Conclusion

The software development lifecycle in GxP-regulated environments is a comprehensive process that requires meticulous planning, execution, and testing. By following the guidelines and best practices outlined in this chapter, including Agile methodologies, companies can develop software that meets regulatory requirements and enhances product quality and patient safety.

4. GxP requirements for software

From a technical perspective, software vendors must adhere to stringent data integrity requirements to ensure compliance in GxP environments:

➢ System administration and access control: Implement robust user authentication and role-based access controls to ensure that only authorized personnel have access to the system.

➢ Audit trails: Develop comprehensive audit trails that automatically record all changes to data, including timestamps, user IDs, and the nature of the changes.

➢ Data backup and recovery: Establish reliable backup solutions and recovery plans. Regularly test these systems to ensure data can be restored quickly and accurately in case of failure.

➢ Electronic records and signatures: Secure electronic records and implement electronic signatures that comply with regulations such as FDA 21 CFR Part 11 and EU Annex 11.

➢ Vendor compliance: Ensure that all third-party vendors comply with GxP regulations. This includes regular audits and assessments of their data security practices.

➢ Network and system security: Protect data integrity through secure network and system configurations, including firewalls, encryption, and intrusion detection systems.

➢ Time synchronization: Ensure all systems use synchronized time sources to maintain accurate time stamps on data.

➢ Data transfers and migrations: Implement secure methods for data transfers and migrations to prevent data corruption or loss.

- ➢ Testing: Conduct thorough testing of software to ensure it meets GxP requirements, including functional testing, performance testing, and security testing.
- ➢ Data integrity monitoring: Use automated tools to continuously monitor data integrity, detecting anomalies or unauthorized changes in real-time.
- ➢ Documentation: Maintain detailed documentation of all processes related to data handling, including development, configuration, testing, maintenance, and decommissioning.

In addition to data integrity, other key GxP requirements include:

- ➢ Training and competency: Ensure that all personnel involved in the development and maintenance of the software system are adequately trained and competent. Regularly update training programs to reflect changes in regulations and technology.
- ➢ Incident management: Implement procedures for identifying, reporting, and resolving incidents that could affect system performance or compliance. This includes root cause analysis and corrective actions.
- ➢ Supplier qualification: Qualify suppliers and vendors to ensure they meet GxP standards. This includes assessing their quality management systems and compliance history.

5. Agile validation

Traditional validation, commonly referred to as Computer System Validation (CSV), is performed by regulated companies using the V-Model to demonstrate compliance.

The V-Model includes structured steps such as validation planning, requirements gathering, risk assessment, testing (often referred to in the pharmaceutical industry as qualification), and validation reporting.

This is a well-established approach, often paper-based—that ensures systems are validated to work as intended and can be reliably used by non-technical users.

Agile validation, by contrast, combines agile software development principles with standard validation practices. It aims to maintain full regulatory compliance while enabling iterative development, faster delivery, and continuous improvement.

There are two scenarios for agile validation:

➤ Regulated companies developing software internally: These companies aim to develop and validate software simultaneously. This approach ensures that the software meets regulatory requirements throughout the development process.
➤ Software development vendors delivering to GxP regulated companies: For these vendors, pre-validating their software based on standard configurations is beneficial from a marketing and sales perspective. It demonstrates compliance and readiness for use in regulated environments.

Regardless of the scenario, understanding how to effectively implement agile validation is crucial. Let's look at the steps involved in agile validation.

5.1. Validation plan

A validation plan in agile validation should include the following key elements:

➢ Scope and objectives: Define the purpose and goals of the validation, including the systems and processes to be validated.
➢ Identify the team members involved in the validation process and their specific roles. Keep in mind the importance of the QA role.
➢ Validation strategy: Outline the approach for validation, including iterative testing and continuous feedback mechanisms.
➢ Risk assessment: Refer to the risk assessment procedure or describe how the risk assessment will be handled.
➢ Test plan: Detail the types of tests to be performed, including functional, performance, and security testing.
➢ Documentation: Specify the documentation required for each phase of validation.
➢ Change control: Refer to the change control procedure or describe how change control will be handled.
➢ Acceptance criteria: Define the criteria for determining whether the system meets validation requirements.
➢ Review and approval: Outline the process for reviewing and approving validation activities and results.

5.2. Requirements definition

A requirements definition for agile validation should include the following key elements:

➢ User requirements: Document the user requirements (can be done in form User Stories), including functional, performance, and security needs. These requirements should be detailed and prioritized based on their importance.
➢ Regulatory requirements: Identify and list all relevant regulatory requirements that the software must comply with. This includes industry standards, guidelines, and specific regulations such as FDA 21 CFR Part 11 and EU Annex 11. It is good practice to create a feature that contains all the requirements (User stories)

5.3. Risk assessment

Conduct a risk assessment to identify potential risks associated with each requirement (user story). This process helps prioritize the main testing areas, ensuring that critical functionalities are thoroughly evaluated. By systematically assessing risks, you can focus resources on the most impactful areas, mitigate potential issues early, and enhance the overall quality and reliability of the software.

5.3.1. Risk assessment method

This method uses two tables to determine risk levels based on severity, probability, and detectability factors.

Probability

		Severity	
Risk Class	Low	Medium	High
High	2	1	1
Medium	3	2	1
Low	3	3	2

Severity – The potential impact on patient safety, product quality, data integrity, or other significant harm, including major business risks.

Probability – The likelihood of the fault occurring.

Risk Class – The product of Severity and Probability (Risk Class = Severity × Probability)

Detectability

Risk	High	Medium	Low
High	Medium	High	High
Medium	Low	Medium	High
Low	Low	Low	Medium

Detectability – The likelihood that the fault will be identified before any harm occurs.

Risk – The product of Risk Class and Detectability (Risk Priority = Risk Class × Detectability

Example

Let's consider a requirement related to audit trail functionality, which falls under the data integrity category. The severity of failure in this area is **high**, and the probability of occurrence is **medium**, resulting in a Risk Class of **1**.

When we reference this **Risk Class** in a secondary assessment table and combine it with a **medium detectability**, the resulting Risk Priority is classified as **high**.

5.4. Risk-based testing

Based on the risk assessment score, determine the intensity of testing required for the software. Higher scores indicate the need for more intensive testing. Prioritize testing efforts on areas related to data integrity, critical processes involved in product manufacturing, and aspects that impact patient health.

5.4.1. Test approach based on risk classification

The test approach based on risk classification should be defined by each company according to its risk appetite and regulatory expectations. Below are a few brief examples of how such an approach might be structured:

● **High risk**

Example: Audit trail, electronic signatures, calculation logic affecting batch release.

Testing approach:

- ➤ Comprehensive positive and negative testing.
- ➤ Boundary and stress tests.
- ➤ Code reviews and peer reviews.
- ➤ Independent verification (e.g., separate test team, QA).
- ➤ 100% test coverage for related requirements.
- ➤ Regression testing for all connected modules.

☐ Medium risk

Example: Role-based access control, data export.

Testing Approach:

- ➤ Adequate positive and key negative tests.
- ➤ Focus on common failure paths.
- ➤ Code reviews and peer reviews.
- ➤ Risk-based regression testing.

☐ Low risk

Example: UI formatting, help text, read-only dashboards.

Testing approach:

- ➤ Positive path testing only.
- ➤ Code review optional but recommended.
- ➤ Group testing with similar low-risk items (e.g., via scripts).
- ➤ Exploratory or informal testing may be sufficient.

> Can be deprioritized if time or resources are constrained.

5.5. Validation report

A validation report on agile validation should include the following key elements:

> Summary of validation activities: Provide an overview of the validation process, including the scope, objectives, and validation strategy.
> Roles and responsibilities: List the team members involved in the validation and their specific roles.
> Test results: Present detailed results of all tests performed, including functional, performance, and security testing. Alternatively, refer to the Qualification Summary Report document to gather all this information.
> Issues and resolutions: Document any issues encountered during validation and the actions taken to resolve them.
> Acceptance criteria: Confirm whether the system meets the predefined acceptance criteria.
> Conclusion: Provide a final assessment of the validation, including a statement that the system works as intended

These elements ensure a thorough and transparent validation report, demonstrating compliance and quality throughout the development lifecycle.

Conclusion

Agile validation offers a robust framework for ensuring compliance, quality, and efficiency in software development for regulated companies and software development firms. By integrating validation activities into the agile development process, organizations can adapt to changing regulations, enhance collaboration, and continuously improve their products. This approach not only ensures regulatory compliance but also delivers high-quality software that meets the needs of both the market and regulatory bodies.

6. Final thoughts

Software development for GxP regulated companies, such as those in the pharmaceutical industry, laboratories, clinical trials, and the broader life sciences sector, has unique requirements. Understanding these specifics is crucial for software vendors and system suppliers to prepare products that fit these industries. In the GxP world, there is a tendency to shift data integrity and cybersecurity responsibilities to vendors, as this is the easiest way to achieve compliance in these areas. Built-in data integrity is a primary requirement that software vendors and system suppliers must comply with when delivering solutions to the pharmaceutical and GxP regulated industry.

7. About the author

Adrian Krzesniak has been involved in software development for the GxP regulated industry since 2007, working in both startups and large technological corporations. He is also a consultant and Udemy trainer in areas such as computer system validation, agile validation, AI in GxP, infrastructure qualification, mobile validation, and Excel spreadsheet validation. Adrian is the author of numerous books on engineering, engineering management, computer system validation, and data integrity in the GxP world.

8. Additional resources

If you would like to learn more about computer system validation, data integrity, and software engineering, check out my courses on Udemy or my books on Amazon. You can find them by searching for "Adrian Krzesniak Udemy" or "Adrian Krzesniak Amazon" on Google.